RENAL DIET COOKBOOK

The Low Sodium, Low Potassium Recipes to Managing Kidney, Liver Disease and Avoiding Dialysis

Marvin Sidwell

Renal Diet Cookbook

© Copyright 2020 by Marvin Sidwell

Renal Diet Cookbook

Contents

ABOUT

People with compromised kidney function must adhere to a renal or kidney diet to cut down on the amount of waste in their blood. Wastes in the blood come from food and liquids that are consumed. When kidney function is compromised, the kidneys not filter or remove waste properly. If waste is left in the blood, it can negatively affect a patient's electrolyte levels. Following a kidney diet may also help promote kidney function and slow the progression of complete kidney failure.

A renal diet is one that is low in sodium, phosphorous, and protein. A renal diet also emphasizes the importance of consuming high-quality protein and usually limiting fluids. Some patients may also need to limit potassium and calcium. Every person's body is different, and therefore, it is crucial that each patient works with a renal dietitian work to come up with a diet that is tailored to the patient's needs.

Read on to learn how to make exciting meals that are crucial to monitor and promote a renal health.

Renal Diet Cookbook

BREAKFAST

1. Instant Pot Steel Cut Oats

Yields:6 Servings

Prep Time:0 Hours 5 Mins

Total Time:0 Hours 40 Mins

Ingredients

- 2 c. steel cut oats
- 3 1/2 c. water
- 2 c. 2% milk
- 1/2 tsp. ground cinnamon
- 1/2 tsp. kosher salt
- 2 tbsp. maple syrup, plus more for serving
- 1 tsp. pure vanilla extract
- Sliced banana, for serving
- Blueberries, for serving
- Toasted sliced almonds, for serving

Renal Diet Cookbook

Directions

1. Combine oats, water, milk, cinnamon, and salt in Instant pot. Press the manual setting and set the cooking time for 5 minutes on high. Let steam release naturally for 20 minutes before flipping the release valve.
2. Remove lid and stir in maple syrup and vanilla. Serve topped with more maple syrup, bananas, blueberries, and almonds.

2. Ham & Cheese Egg Cups

Yields:12

Prep Time:0 Hours 5 Mins

Cook Time:0 Hours 0 Mins

Total Time:0 Hours 5 Mins

Ingredients

- Cooking spray, for pan
- 12 slices ham
- 1 c. shredded cheddar
- 12 large eggs
- Kosher salt
- Freshly ground black pepper
- Chopped fresh parsley, for garnish

Directions

1. Preheat oven to 400º and grease a 12-cup muffin tin with cooking spray. Line each cup with a slice of ham and sprinkle with cheddar. Crack an egg into each ham cup and season with salt and pepper.

2. Bake until eggs are cooked through, 12 to 15 minutes (depending on how runny you like your yolks).
3. Garnish with parsley and serve.

Yields:15 Servings
Prep Time:0 Hours 10 Mins
Total Time:0 Hours 50 Mins

Ingredients

- 1 c. all-purpose flour
- 1/2 whole wheat flour
- 1 tsp. baking powder
- 1/2 tsp. baking soda
- 1/2 tsp. kosher salt
- 2 tsp. pumpkin pie spice
- 1 c. canned pumpkin
- 1/2 c. honey
- 2 large eggs
- 6 tbsp. butter, melted and cooled
- 1/4 c. Greek yogurt
- 1 c. toasted and chopped pecans
- 2 tbsp. Demerara sugar

Directions

1. Preheat oven to 325° and line muffin tin with liners.
2. In a large bowl, whisk together flours, baking powder, baking soda, salt, and pumpkin pie spice. Add pumpkin, honey, eggs, butter, and yogurt, and mix until combined. Fold in 3/4 cup pecans.
3. Divide batter into muffin liners, then top with remaining pecans and Demerara sugar. Bake until muffins are golden brown and a toothpick comes out clean, about 30 minutes. Let muffins cool in pan, then serve.

4. Avocado Egg Boats

Yields:4 Servings

Prep Time:0 Hours 10 Mins

Total Time:0 Hours 40 Mins

Ingredients

2 ripe avocados, halved and pitted

4 large eggs

Kosher salt

Freshly ground black pepper

3 slices bacon

Freshly chopped chives, for garnish

Directions

1. Preheat oven to 350°. Scoop about 1 tablespoon worth of avocado out of each half; discard or reserve for another use.
2. Place hollowed avocados in a baking dish, then crack eggs into a bowl, one at a time. Using a spoon, transfer one yolk to each avocado half, then spoon in as much egg white as you can fit without spilling over.

3. Season with salt and pepper and bake until whites are set and yolks are no longer runny, 20 to 25 minutes. (Cover with foil if avocados are beginning to brown.)
4. Meanwhile, in a large skillet over medium heat, cook bacon until crisp, 8 minutes, then transfer to a paper towel-lined plate and chop.
5. Top avocados with bacon and chives before serving.

5. Instant Pot Yogurt

Yields:2 Quarts

Prep Time:0 Hours 5 Mins

Total Time:12 Hours 45 Mins

Ingredients

- 2 qt. whole milk
- 2 tbsp. whole-milk Greek yogurt

Directions

1. Pour milk into a 6-quart Instant Pot and lock lid. Press the Yogurt setting until it reads "boil". This cycle will take about 35 minutes.
2. Follow manufacturer's guide for quick release, making sure to wait until cycle is complete before unlocking and removing lid. Check that the milk temperature is at least 180°. If less than 180°, repeat the boil cycle. If 180° or higher, remove inner pot and cool milk in an ice bath to between 110° and 115°, checking frequently with an instant read thermometer, 4 to 5 minutes.

3. Once milk is 110° to 115°, place Greek yogurt in a medium bowl, then remove about a cup of milk and whisk into yogurt. Whisk yogurt mixture back into Instant Pot until fully incorporated, then lock lid and press the Yogurt setting to Normal for 8 to 12 hours. 12 hours will make a thicker yogurt.
4. Remove lid and transfer yogurt to clean containers. Chill until completely set, about 4 hours.

Yields:4 Servings

Prep Time:0 Hours 10 Mins

Total Time:0 Hours 40 Mins

Ingredients

- 6 slices bacon, cut into 1" pieces
- 1/2 onion, chopped
- 1 lb. brussels sprouts, trimmed and quartered
- Kosher salt
- Freshly ground black pepper
- 1/4 tsp. crushed red pepper flakes
- 2 cloves garlic, minced
- 4 large eggs

Directions

1. In a large skillet over medium heat, cook bacon until crispy. Turn off heat and transfer bacon to a paper towel-lined plate. Keep most of bacon fat in skillet, removing any black pieces from pan.

2. Turn heat back to medium and add onion and brussels sprouts to the skillet. Cook, stirring occasionally, until vegetables begin to soften and

turn golden. Season with salt, pepper, and red pepper flakes.

3. Add 2 tablespoons of water and cover skillet. Cook until brussels sprouts are tender and water has evaporated, about 5 minutes. (If all the water evaporates before the brussels sprouts are tender, add more water to skillet and cover for a couple minutes more.) Add garlic to skillet and cook until fragrant, 1 minute.

4. Using a wooden spoon, make four holes in the hash to reveal bottom of skillet. Crack an egg into each hole and season each egg with salt and pepper. Replace lid and cook until eggs are cooked to your liking, about 5 minutes for a just runny egg.

5. Sprinkle cooked bacon bits over entire skillet and serve warm.

Yields:6 Servings

Prep Time:0 Hours 20 Mins

Total Time:0 Hours 40 Mins

Ingredients

- 1 tbsp. butter
- 8 oz. cremini mushrooms, thinly sliced
- 1 shallot, minced
- 2 c. loosely packed spinach
- Kosher salt
- Freshly ground black pepper
- 8 large eggs
- 1/4 c. whole milk
- 1/4 c. oil-packed sun-dried tomatoes, finely chopped
- 1/4 c. freshly grated Parmesan

Directions

1. Preheat oven to 375°. In a medium skillet over medium heat, melt butter. Add mushrooms and let cook, undisturbed, for 2 minutes. Stir and continue

to cook until mushrooms are tender and golden, 5 to 6 minutes. Add shallot and cook until fragrant, 1 minute. Add spinach and cook until wilted, 1 minute more. Season with salt and pepper and remove from heat.

2. In a large bowl, whisk together eggs, milk, tomatoes, and Parmesan. Fold in the mushroom mixture and season again with salt and pepper. Pour into a 8" to 9" pie dish and bake until eggs are just set, 18 to 20 minutes. Let cool 3 minutes before slicing and serving.

8. Instant Pot Hash

Yields:6 Servings

Prep Time:0 Hours 15 Mins

Total Time:0 Hours 50 Mins

Ingredients

- 1 tbsp. extra-virgin olive oil
- 1 tbsp. butter
- 1/2 lb. thick-cut Canadian bacon
- 1/2 medium yellow onion, chopped
- 1 red bell pepper, chopped
- 1 green bell pepper, chopped
- 2 cloves garlic, minced
- 1 tsp. dried oregano
- 1/2 tsp.
- cumin seeds (optional)
- 1/4 tsp. cayenne
- Kosher salt
- Freshly ground black pepper
- 1 lb. yellow potatoes, quartered
- 1/2 c. low-sodium vegetable broth
- 1 tbsp. freshly chopped parsley, for garnish

- Eggs, for serving

Directions

1. Set Instant Pot to Sauté on medium. Add oil and butter to pot. When butter is melted, cook bacon until crisp. Add onions and peppers, and cook until vegetables are tender.
2. Add garlic, oregano, cumin seeds if using, and cayenne. Season with salt and pepper and cook until spices and garlic are fragrant, 1 minute.
3. Add potatoes and broth to pot and stir to combine. Set Instant Pot to Pressure Cook on high and set timer for 12 minutes. When time is up, use quick release method to release pressure.
4. Remove lid and set Instant Pot back on Sauté. Cook, stirring occasionally, until remaining broth is evaporated, about 2 minutes.
5. Garnish with parsley and serve with fried eggs.

Yields:2 Servings

Prep Time:0 Hours 15 Mins

Total Time:0 Hours 30 Mins

Ingredients

- 4 large eggs, separated
- 2 ripe bananas, mashed (about 1 c.)
- 1 c. almond flour
- 3 tbsp. coconut flour
- 1 tsp. baking powder
- 1/4 tsp. ground cinnamon (optional)
- Pinch kosher salt
- Cooking spray
- Butter, for serving
- Maple syrup, for serving
- Berries, for serving

Directions

1. In a large bowl, whisk together egg yolks, bananas, almond flour, coconut flour, baking powder, cinnamon, (if using) and salt. In a separate large

bowl using a hand or standing mixer, whip egg whites until stiff peaks form, 4 to 5 minutes.

2. Gently fold whipped egg whites into batter until evenly combined.

3. Grease a large nonstick pan with cooking spray and place over medium-low heat. Pour about 1/4-cup pancake batter onto the pan, spreading it out evenly. Cook until both sides are lightly golden. Serve with butter, maple syrup, and berries.

10. Ham & Cheese Breakfast Roll-Ups

Yields:2

Prep Time:0 Hours 20 Mins

Total Time:0 Hours 20 Mins

Ingredients

- 4 large eggs
- 1/4 c. milk
- 2 tbsp. Chopped chives
- kosher salt
- Freshly ground black pepper
- 1 tbsp. butter
- 1 c. shredded cheddar, divided
- 4 slices ham

Directions

1. In a medium bowl, whisk together eggs, milk, and chives. Season with salt and pepper.
2. In a medium skillet over medium heat, melt butter. Pour half of the egg mixture into the skillet, moving to create a thin layer that covers the entire pan.

3. Cook for 2 minutes. Add 1/2 cup cheddar and cover for 2 minutes more, until the cheese is melty. Remove onto plate, place 2 slices of ham, and roll tightly. Repeat with remaining ingredients and serve.

LUNCH

11. Pesto Pasta Salad with Sun Dried Tomatoes

Prep Time: 5 mins

Cook Time: 10 mins

Yield: 8

Ingredients

- 1 16 oz box cellentani, rotini, or bowtie pasta
- 1 cup pesto sauce
- 1 can chickpeas
- ½ cup sun-dried tomatoes chopped
- ½ cup shredded parmesan cheese
- 1 head broccoli florets
- 1 tbsp olive oil
- Salt and pepper to taste
- ½ lemon (optional)

Directions

1. Heat the oven to 400 degrees F. Wash and dry the broccoli, then cut into small florets. Arrange in a single layer on a baking sheet and drizzle

with the olive oil. Season with salt and pepper to taste. Roast 10 minutes on high heat or until the edges begin to brown and the broccoli is cooked to your preference.

2. While the oven is preheating, bring a large pot of water to a boil. Once boiling, add the pasta and cook until al dente, about 8-10 minutes depending on your pasta shape.

3. Meanwhile, chop the sun-dried tomatoes and drain and rinse the chickpeas. Set aside until ready to combine.

4. Once pasta is cooked, drain and add to a large mixing bowl. Remove the broccoli from the oven and allow to cool slightly. Add to the mixing bowl with the pesto sauce, sun-dried tomatoes, and chickpeas. If using lemon, squeeze over the top, being careful not to include the seeds. Gently fold together to combine all ingredients.

5. Top with parmesan cheese just before serving. Serve warm, or chill until ready to serve.

12. Quick & Easy Toasted Za'atar Chickpea Gyros

Cook Time: 20

Servings: 6-8

Ingredients

- 1.5 cup – Garbanzo Beans, low-sodium
- 8 Pita Pockets
- 4 oz – Goat Cheese
- 2 – Roma/Plum Tomato
- 6 leaves – Lettuce, Romaine Hearts
- 1 tablespoon – Za'atar Spice
- 1 tsp – Extra Virgin Olive Oil
- 2 tsp – Dill Weed
- 1 fruit – Lemon, raw
- ½ cup – Cucumber, raw

Directions

1. Preheat oven to 425°F.

Toasted Garbanzos

2. Drain garbanzo beans and pat dry. In bowl, combine garbanzos, olive oil, and za'atar. Toss to coat well.
3. Spread into sheet tray lined with parchment.
4. Toast in oven 425°F approximately 20 minutes.
5. Turning occasionally, until dark and crispy, but don't let bean get hard and dried out. Remove and set aside.

Goat Cheese Spread

6. Combine goat cheese with dill. Mix well. Squeeze lemon and add to taste.

Gyro

7. Spread goat cheese onto pita. Top with toasted garbanzos.
8. Add sliced tomato, sliced cucumber, and romaine.

13. Kale and KORU Apple Salad

Prep Time: 15 mins

Yield: 6

Ingredients

Salad

- 8 cups baby kale (or spinach)
- 2 medium KORU apples, cored and thinly sliced
- ½ cup dried cranberries
- ½ cup cucumber, thinly sliced
- 1 small red onion, thinly sliced

Salad Dressing

- ¼ cup extra virgin olive oil
- 2 tablespoons apple cider vinegar
- 1 tablespoon honey (or maple syrup)
- 1 teaspoon Dijon mustard
- Sea salt and ground pepper to taste

Topping

- ½ cup
  slivered almonds, pecan or walnut halves,
  toasted
- 4 ounces feta cheese, crumbled

Directions

Salad

1. Toss salad ingredients together in a large salad bowl.
2. For the dressing, place all ingredients in a jar and shake well to mix.
3. Drizzle salad dressing over salad and toss lightly.
4. Sprinkle with almonds and feta cheese over the top.
5. Salad should be served shortly after adding the dressing.

Salad Dressing

1. Mix ingredients in a bowl

Topping

1. Mix ingredients in a bowl

14. Apple Cranberry Holiday Stuffing with Arctic Apples

Prep Time: 15 mins

Yields: 8

Ingredients

- 10 cups sourdough bread about one loaf, cubed
- 1 stick unsalted butter
- 2 ribs celery
- ½ yellow onion
- 1 large Arctic® Granny or Arctic® Golden apple, or 8 ounces of fresh slices
- 1 cup fresh cranberries
- 2 ½ cups low sodium vegetable stock
- salt and pepper to taste
- 2 large eggs
- 2 tbsp fresh parsley chopped
- 2 tbsp fresh sage chopped
- 1 tbsp fresh rosemary chopped
- 1 tbsp fresh thyme chopped

- nonstick cooking spray

Directions

1. If using a fresh loaf of sourdough bread, cube or tear into small pieces the evening before. Arrange on a baking sheet and allow to stale overnight.
2. Preheat oven to 350 degrees F and prepare a large casserole dish with nonstick cooking spray or oil.
3. In a large skillet, melt the butter over medium-high heat. Prepare the celery by slicing down the middle of each rib, then chopping into a small dice. Dice the onion, then add both to the skillet with the butter. Season with salt and pepper and allow to cook until translucent and fragrant, about 5 to 6 minutes.
4. Meanwhile, chop the fresh herbs and add to a large mixing bowl with the sourdough bread. Dice the apple, then add to the mixing bowl along with the fresh cranberries. Pour half of the vegetable stock over the mixture and fold together to combine.

5. Whisk the eggs into the remaining vegetable stock. When the onion-celery mixture is ready, add to the mixing bowl. Fold to combine, then pour the remaining liquid over the top.

6. Transfer to the prepared casserole dish and spread in an even layer. Top with additional herbs if desired, and season lightly with salt and pepper. Cover with foil and bake 30 minutes.

7. After 30 minutes, remove the foil and return to the oven to bake 10 to 15 minutes more, or until the top begins to brown. Allow to cool slightly before serving, and garnish with additional herbs if desired. Serve immediately, or hold warm until ready to serve.

Prep Time: 1 hr

Yields: 6

Ingredients

- 1 Tbsp butter
- 1 medium sweet yellow onion, diced
- 3 cups thinly sliced zucchini
- 1 can (15 oz.) Libby's® Whole Kernel Sweet Corn, drained
- 4 eggs, beaten
- ½ cup shredded Monterey Jack cheese
- 1/2 cup shredded mozzarella cheese
- 2 tsp dried oregano
- 1 tsp dried basil
- 1 tsp chili powder
- 1/2 tsp salt
- 1/2 tsp cracked black pepper

Directions

1. Preheat oven to 375 degrees F. Melt butter in large skillet over medium-high heat. Add onion

and zucchini; sauté for 5-7 minutes. Stir in Libby's Whole Kernel Sweet Corn and continue to cook until zucchini is fully softened, around 2 minutes more. Remove from heat and drain excess liquid. Let cool.

2. Whisk eggs in large bowl then stir in cheese and seasonings. Gently fold cooled vegetables into egg and cheese mixture.

3. Line 8-inch pie pan with parchment paper and transfer mixture to pan, arranging the top so zucchini slices lay in single, flat layer. Cover with foil and bake 25 minutes.

4. Remove foil and bake for additional 10 minutes until top is browned. Let stand for 10-15 minutes before cutting into slices.

16. Halos Mandarins and Beet Holiday Salad

Prep Time: 1 hr 15 mins

Yields: 4

Ingredients

- 1 teaspoon Dijon mustard
- Freshly ground black pepper
- 2 tablespoons sherry vinegar
- 3/4 cup good quality olive oil
- Pinch of salt

Directions

1. Preheat oven to 375°F.
2. Cut tops and bottoms off beets.
3. Place beets on sheet pan with a little water, cover with aluminum foil, and bake for 1 hour or more, until easily pierced with a knife.
4. Cool until just warm, and peel off skin.
5. Slice into sections or any shape you like. Now they're ready to add color to your salad!

17. Quinoa Salad with Corn and Peas

Prep Time: 20 mins

Yields: 4

Ingredients

- 1 cup uncooked quinoa
- 2 cups water
- 1 can (15 oz.) Libby's® Whole Kernel Sweet Corn, drained
- 1 can (15 oz.) Libby's® Sweet Peas, drained
- 1/2 cup diced red onion
- 2 large tomatoes, seeded and diced
- 4 oz. fresh mozzarella, diced
- 1/8 cup chopped fresh parsley
- 1 Tbsp lemon juice
- 2 Tbsp olive oil

Directions

1. Add quinoa and water to medium pot and bring it to a boil. Cover, then reduce heat to simmer and cook 15 minutes. Remove from heat and let

sit covered for 5 minutes. Place into large bowl and fluff with fork. Let cool.

2. Add corn, peas, onions, tomato, cheese, parsley, lime juice and olive oil. Gently toss mixture until combined.

18. Southern Green Beans and New Potatoes with Bacon

Ingredients

- 4-5 slices hickorysmoked bacon
- 1 teaspoon butter
- 2 cloves garlic, minced
- 2 shallots, chopped
- 1 pound new potatoes, boiled until tender
- 1 family size frozen French cut green beans, defrosted and drained
- Sea salt and ground black pepper to taste
- 1 teaspoon dried parsley
- 1 teaspoon dried rosemary

Directions

1. Remove the outer skin from the garlic and shallots. Wash the potatoes, garlic and shallots: rub by hand or scrub with a clean brush while rinsing under running tap water. Dry with a clean cloth towel or paper towel before cutting vegetables.

2. Fill a large cooking pot with water, at least 2 inches above the potatoes, and drop in the potatoes. Add 1 tablespoon of salt and allow the potatoes to boil on high heat. Boil until the potatoes are tender, about 25 minutes. Using a colander, drain the potatoes, and rinse with cold water. Set aside.

3. Slice bacon into bite size pieces. Heat the skillet. When hot, add sliced bacon. After handling the bacon, wash your hands and the cutting board with hot, soapy water.

4. Cook bacon until crispy. Place the cooked bacon on a paper towel to drain. Remove the skillet from the heat and spoon out half of the leftover bacon grease. Allow the grease to cool and discard.

5. Turn down the heat to medium-low. Add 1 teaspoon of butter to the skillet. When the butter is melted, add minced garlic and chopped shallots. Sauté for 20-30 seconds.

6. Add tender new potatoes, and turn a few times so the skin of the potatoes is coated with the oil.

7. Gently stir the green beans together with the potatoes in the skillet. Season with sea salt and ground black pepper, dried parsley and rosemary. Crumble the cooked bacon on top of the mixture. Continue heating and stir occasionally until a food thermometer reads 165 ºF and the dish is steaming. Serve immediately.

8. Store leftovers in shallow containers within 2 hours of serving. Leftovers will last in the refrigerator up to 3-4 days.

19. Holiday Cobb Salad

Prep Time: 20 mins

Yields: 6

Ingredients

- 1 pkg. (9 oz.) DOLE Hearts of Romaine
- Apple-Bleu Cheese Vinaigrette (see recipe below)
- 2 cups cubed roasted turkey
- 2 cups cooked DOLE Brussels Sprouts, sliced
- 2 cups cooked DOLE Sweet Potatoes
- 1 large tomato, cored and cut into
- ½-inch pieces 1 avocado, peeled, pitted, and diced
- 1 DOLE Apple, cored and cut into ½-inch pieces
- 1 cup DOLE Blackberries

Directions

1. Toss Hearts of Romaine with Apple-Bleu Cheese Vinaigrette.
2. Arrange romaine on large serving plate. Arrange turkey, Brussels sprouts, sweet

potatoes, tomatoes, avocado, apple and blackberries in long, narrow rows on top of the romaine.

20. Tomato Spinach Salad with Red Pepper Dressing
Servings: 2

Ingredients

- 2 cups spinach
- 2 cups lettuce or baby greens
- 1 medium tomato, cut into chunks
- 1 red pepper, seeded
- 1 orange, peeled
- 1 cup cucumber slices, cut in half circles
- ¼ cup sundried tomatoes
- ½ cup feta cheese, cut into small chunks

Red Pepper Dressing

- 1 roasted red pepper, cut in small pieces
- 1 tbsp white onion, chopped in to small pieces
- 2 tbsp olive oil
- 1 ½ tbsp apple cider vinegar
- 1 tbsp fresh parsley

- ½ tsp mustard
- 1 tsp raw honey
- Sea salt (or table salt) and pepper to taste

Directions

1. Place the spinach, lettuce green, red pepper and tomatoes into a bowl.
2. Peel the orange apart into wedges and cut the wedges into three pieces. Remove any seeds. Add to the bowl along with the cucumber slices, sundried tomatoes and the feta cheese.
3. Make the red pepper dressing by placing all the ingredients in a blender and blend.
4. Pour the dressing on the salad and toss. Adjust to taste with sea salt and pepper, if needed. Serve.

DINNER

21. Cheesy Ground Beef Tacos

Yields:8

Prep Time:0 Hours 10 Mins

Total Time:0 Hours 25 Mins

Ingredients

- 1 large onion, chopped
- 1 lb. ground beef
- 1 (15-oz.) can fire-roasted tomatoes
- 1 (15-oz.) can black beans, drained and rinsed
- 1 tbsp. taco seasoning
- kosher salt2 c. shredded cheddar or pepper jack
- 8 Small flour tortillas
- Sliced green onions, for serving
- Sour cream, for serving

Directions

1. In a large skillet over medium-high heat, cook onion until soft, 6 minutes. Add beef and cook until

no longer pink, 5 to 7 minutes more, then add tomatoes, black beans, and taco seasoning and season with salt. Stir until combined. Add cheese and stir until completely melted.

2. Spoon mixture into flour tortillas and fold. Garnish with green onions and serve with sour cream.

Yields:4 Servings

Prep Time:0 Hours 5 Mins

Total Time:0 Hours 40 Mins

Ingredients

- 1 tbsp. extra-virgin olive oil
- 4 boneless skinless chicken breasts
- Kosher salt
- Freshly ground black pepper
- 1 tsp. dried oregano
- 3 tbsp. butter
- 3 cloves garlic, minced
- 1 1/2 c. cherry tomatoes, halved
- 3 c. baby spinach
- 1/2 c. heavy cream
- 1/4 c. freshly grated Parmesan
- Lemon wedges, for serving

Directions

1. In a skillet over medium heat, heat oil. Add chicken and season with salt, pepper, and oregano. Cook until golden and no longer pink, 8 minutes per side. Remove from skillet and set aside.

2. In the same skillet over medium heat, melt butter. Stir in garlic and cook until fragrant, about 1 minute. Add cherry tomatoes and season with salt and pepper. Cook until tomatoes are beginning to burst then add spinach and cook until spinach is beginning to wilt.

3. Stir in heavy cream and parmesan and bring mixture to a simmer. Reduce heat to low and simmer until sauce is slightly reduced, about 3 minutes. Return chicken to skillet and cook until heated through, 5 to 7 minutes.

4. Serve with lemon wedges.

Yields:4 Servings

Prep Time:0 Hours 10 Mins

Cook Time:0 Hours 20 Mins

Total Time:0 Hours 30 Mins

Ingredients

- 1 1/2 lb. ground beef
- 2 c. shredded Mexican cheese blend, divided
- 1/2 c. panko bread crumbs
- 2 tbsp. freshly chopped parsley, plus more for garnish
- 2 cloves garlic, minced
- 1 jalapeño, finely chopped
- 1 large egg
- 1 tsp. ground cumin
- Kosher salt
- Freshly ground black pepper
- 1 tbsp. extra-virgin olive oil
- 1/2 large onion, chopped
- 1 (15-oz.) can crushed tomatoes
- 2 tbsp. chopped chipotle chiles in adobo sauce

Directions

1. In a medium bowl, combine ground beef, 1 cup of cheese, bread crumbs, parsley, garlic, jalapeño, egg, and cumin and season with salt and pepper. Mix until combined, then form into meatballs.
2. In a large skillet over medium-high heat, heat oil. Add meatballs in a single layer and sear 2 minutes per side. Transfer to a plate.
3. Add onion to skillet and cook, stirring, until soft, 5 minutes. Stir in crushed tomatoes and chipotle in adobo and bring mixture to a boil. Reduce heat to medium-low and return meatballs to skillet. Cover and simmer until meatballs are cooked through, about 10 minutes.
4. Top with remaining 1 cup cheese, then cover with lid to let melt, about 2 minutes.
5. Garnish with parsley before serving.

Yields:4 Servings

Prep Time:0 Hours 15 Mins

Total Time:0 Hours 50 Mins

Ingredients

- 4 boneless skinless chicken breasts
- Kosher salt
- Freshly ground black pepper
- 4 oz. cream cheese, softened
- 1/2 c. frozen spinach, defrosted and drained
- 1/3 c. chopped artichoke hearts
- 1 c. shredded mozzarella, divided
- Pinch crushed red pepper flakes
- 4 strips bacon, cut into 4 strips
- 2 tbsp. extra-virgin olive oil

Directions

1. Preheat oven to 400°. Line a large baking sheet with foil. Make slits widthwise in chicken, being careful not to cut all the way through chicken.

Season with salt and pepper. Place on prepared baking sheet.

2. In a medium bowl, combine cream cheese, spinach, artichokes, and ½ cup of mozzarella. Season with salt, pepper, and a pinch of red pepper flakes. Fill every other slit with cream cheese mixture and fill remaining slits with a piece of bacon. Sprinkle remaining ½ cup mozzarella on top and drizzle with oil.

3. Bake until chicken is cooked through and bacon is crispy, 35 minutes.

25. Oven-Fried Chicken

Yields:4 Servings

Prep Time:0 Hours 15 Mins

Total Time:1 Hour 15 Mins

Ingredients

For The Chicken

- 2 c. panko bread crumbs
- 1/2 tsp. garlic powder
- Kosher salt
- Freshly ground black pepper
- 3 large eggs
- 1/4 c. buttermilk
- 6 bone-in, skin-on chicken thighs

For The Dipping Sauce

- 3 tbsp. Dijon mustard
- 2 tbsp. barbecue sauce
- 1 tbsp. mayonnaise
- 2 tsp. honey

Directions

1. Preheat oven to 425°. Line a baking sheet with aluminum foil. In a medium bowl, mix together panko bread crumbs and garlic powder and season with salt and pepper.
2. In another medium bowl, whisk together eggs and buttermilk.
3. Pat thighs dry, then dip into egg mixture, then dredge in panko, making sure all sides are completely coated. Place on prepared baking sheet and bake until golden and crispy, and a thermometer inserted in the center reads 180°, about 1 hour.
4. Make dipping sauce: In a large bowl, whisk together Dijon, barbecue sauce, mayonnaise, and honey.
5. Serve chicken with dipping sauce.

Yields:4

Prep Time:0 Hours 5 Mins

Cook Time:0 Hours 20 Mins

Total Time:0 Hours 25 Mins

Ingredients

- 2 cloves garlic
- 1/2 c. peanut butter
- 1/4 c. soy sauce
- 1/4 c. water
- 2 tbsp. honey
- Juice of 1 lemon
- kosher salt
- Freshly ground black pepper
- 1 tbsp. vegetable oil
- 1 red pepper, sliced
- 1 yellow pepper, sliced
- 1 red onion, thinly sliced
- 1 head broccoli, florets only
- 2 c. green beans, trimmed
- 2 c. carrots, sliced into half moons

- 1 pkg. cooked soba noodles

Directions

1. In a medium bowl, combine garlic, peanut butter, soy sauce, water, honey, and lemon juice and whisk until smooth. Season with salt and pepper.
2. Heat a large skillet over medium-high heat and add vegetable oil. Cook onions, carrots, broccoli, peppers, and green beans until tender but still vibrant, about 10 minutes.
3. To skillet, add cooked soba noodles and stir to combine. Serve!

27. Skinny Orange Chicken

Yields:4

Prep Time:0 Hours 20 Mins

Total Time:0 Hours 40 Mins

Ingredients

- 2 c. all-purpose flour
- 2 large Eggs, beaten
- 2 c. panko bread crumbs
- 1 lb. boneless skinless chicken breasts, cut into chunks
- kosher salt
- Freshly ground black pepper
- Juice and zest of 2 oranges
- 1/3 c. low-sodium soy sauce
- 1/4 c. honey
- 2 cloves garlic, minced
- 2 tsp. freshly grated ginger
- 2 tbsp. cornstarch
- 2 c. cooked jasmine rice
- Sesame seeds, for garnish
- Sliced green onions, for garnish

Directions

1. Preheat oven to 400° and line a baking sheet with parchment.
2. Set up a dredging station with one bowl of flour, one of eggs, and one of panko. Dredge the chicken in flour, then coat in eggs and cover in panko. Season generously with salt and pepper.
3. Arrange chicken on parchment-lined baking sheet and bake until no longer pink, 18 to 20 minutes.
4. Meanwhile, make sauce: In a small saucepan over medium heat, combine orange juice, soy sauce, honey, garlic, ginger, and cornstarch. Whisk until combined and cook until thickened, about 5 minutes.
5. Transfer chicken to a large bowl and toss in orange sauce.
6. Serve over rice with orange zest, sesame seeds, and green onions.

28. Turkey Taco Lettuce Wraps

Yields:4 Servings

Prep Time:0 Hours 5 Mins

Total Time:0 Hours 20 Mins

Ingredients

- 2 tbsp. extra-virgin olive oil
- 1 small yellow onion, chopped
- 1 lb. ground turkey
- 1 tsp. kosher salt
- 1 tbsp. tomato paste
- 1 tbsp. chili powder
- 1 c. low-sodium chicken broth
- 2 heads romaine lettuce, outer leaves separated
- Shredded Mexican cheese, for serving

For Serving
- Shredded Mexican cheese
- Chopped tomatoes
- Chopped red onion
- Chopped avocado
- Freshly chopped cilantro

Renal Diet Cookbook

Directions

1. Heat oil in a large skillet over medium-high. Add onion and cook until just soft, about 5 minutes. Add turkey and season with salt. Cook, breaking up meat with the side of a spoon, until meat is cooked through, 4 minutes.
2. Stir in tomato paste and chili powder and cook 1 minute. Add broth and simmer, stirring occasionally, until thickened, about 2 minutes more.
3. Double up lettuce leaves. Divide meat mixture among leaves. Sprinkle with cheese, tomato, onion, avocado, and cilantro and serve.

29. Egg Roll Bowls

Yields:4

Prep Time:0 Hours 10 Mins

Total Time:0 Hours 35 Mins

Ingredients

- 1 tbsp. vegetable oil
- 1 clove garlic, minced
- 1 tbsp. minced fresh ginger
- 1 lb. ground pork
- 1 tbsp. sesame oil
- 1/2 onion, thinly sliced
- 1 c. shredded carrot
- 1/4 green cabbage, thinly sliced
- 1/4 c. soy sauce
- 1 tbsp. Sriracha
- 1 green onion, thinly sliced
- 1 tbsp. sesame seeds

Directions

1. In a large skillet over medium heat, heat vegetable oil. Add garlic and ginger and cook until fragrant, 1 to 2 minutes. Add pork and cook until no pink remains.
2. Push pork to the side and add sesame oil. Add onion, carrot, and cabbage. Stir to combine with meat and add soy sauce and Sriracha. Cook until cabbage is tender, 5 to 8 minutes.
3. Transfer mixture to a serving dish and garnish with green onions and sesame seeds. Serve.

30. Buffalo Chicken-Stuffed Peppers

Yields:4

Prep Time:0 Hours 20 Mins

Total Time:0 Hours 40 Mins

Ingredients

- 4 bell peppers, halved, seeds and cores removed
- 1 tbsp. extra-virgin olive oil
- Kosher salt
- Freshly ground black pepper
- 3 tbsp. butter
- 1/2 large onion, chopped
- 2 cloves garlic
- 3 c. shredded rotisserie chicken
- 1/2 c. hot sauce (preferably Frank's Red Hot)
- 2 c. shredded Gouda
- Ranch dressing, for drizzling
- 2 tbsp. freshly chopped chives

Directions

1. Preheat oven to 400°. Place bell peppers cut side up on a large baking sheet and drizzle all over with olive oil, then season with salt and pepper.
2. In a large skillet over medium heat, melt butter. Add onion and cook until tender, about 5 minutes. Add garlic and cook until fragrant, 1 minute more.
3. Add shredded chicken and hot sauce and toss until combined. Cook until the mixture comes to a simmer, then remove from heat.
4. Divide chicken mixture between pepper halves. Top with Gouda and bake until cheese is melted and peppers are crisp-tender, 20 to 25 minutes.
5. Drizzle each stuffed pepper with ranch dressing and sprinkle with chives.

Made in the USA
Las Vegas, NV
14 April 2024

88666388R00038